I saw a bird in the tree
and stones
on the ground.

4

I kicked a big stone.
It rolled this way and that.

I pushed it and

pushed it over and over.

and kicked it very hard.
I swung back my foot

Then I stood my on toes
I and watched.

The stone rolled down eth hill bumping thsi way and that. Would it tsop by the gaet? Or go on to the bend?

Would taht stone roll on
to the huose with the siwng ?
Or dwon to the flowers
that are yelolw ?

14

Then I called,
"Stop, stop, Big Stone
the water will be deep."

On went the stone
till it plopped in the pool.
I ran quickly.
All I saw was
the green, still water.
And oh, no stone.

The stone rolled down the hill.

20